LOCK HER UP

LOCK HER UP

by
Tina Parker

Accents Publishing • Lexington, Kentucky • 2021

Printed in the United States of America

Accents Publishing
Editor: Katerina Stoykova-Klemer
Cover Image: *Sloughing Off* by Shari Weschler
Patient Record Image: Courtesy of the Library of Virginia

Library of Congress Control Number: 2021935236
ISBN: 978-1-936628-65-0
First Edition

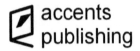

Accents Publishing is an independent press for brilliant voices. For a catalog of current and upcoming titles, please visit us on the Web at

www.accents-publishing.com

CONTENTS

Part Three: Release

THE DAY THEY CAME FOR ME

I sliced open the sun
I walked the tight rope
And touched the moon

I drank stars that day
I danced with a tree
Climbed into thunder

The day they came for me
I cartwheeled into the sea
And sang open the snow.

Part One: Admission

Women were particularly susceptible to insanity caused by pregnancy, childbirth, seduction, menstrual problems, too-tight corsets, and reading works of fiction.

—The Perception and Treatment of Insanity in Southern Appalachia

PLEAS FOR ADMISSION

Will you take my mother
> She is widowed, violent, vulgar, she eats too much and chaws tobacco

Will you take my daughter
> She is wild, incoherent, frolicsome, and restless

Will you take my wife
> She is lazy, obstinate, indisposed, and takes no interest in her home

Will you take my wife
> She complains a great deal, but most of her suffering is imaginary

Will you take my daughter
> She is a constant aberration

Will you take my mother
> She has done nothing for the past 10 or 15 years but sit and deplore her condition.

STATE OF VIRGINIA
County or City of

_____ *Smyth* _____

REPORT OF COMMISSION
Regarding the
INSANITY
——OF——

_____ *Mattie M. Roberts* _____

Date of Certificate

_____ *May 29* _____ 19____

I have good reasons to suspect that Mattie M. Roberts is a Lunatic and ought to be committed to an asylum these are therefore to command you in the name of the Commonwealth forthwith to the lady of the said Miss Mattie Roberts, age 19 years, daughter of E. H. Roberts, and bring her to me at Harvey's store in the Said County on the 5th day of June that she May be Examined touching her Lunacy and to be farther proceeded with according to law and you are further summoned Dr. Terrell and Rev. Harris to attend at the same time and place as witnesses to testify touching the Lunacy of the said Miss Mattie Roberts.

TESTIMONY

They told the judge
I sat before an open fire
Fell right into it
But wasn't a hair on my head singed.

They recalled my vision
A prophetess wearing clothes
The color of rotten grasses
Grounding sage to a fine powder
They said I put it in their tea
Told them to drink
And be sanctified
Said their throats burned
Claimed they could not speak.

The minister said he'd seen many
Slain in the spirit but not me
Said I was different
That he felt directed to sign
As witness.

THE INCIDENT: NIGHT

I found the bloodied sheet
At the fence line
Behind our house
Pulled clumps of matted
Hair from the sink
Each time I dozed off
A hand slapped my cheek.

THERE IS ROOM

They examined it
said it was full   things in there I cannot
name
the first a ring
the second an apron

no
the first was an apron
and undershirts
gowns slippers
dresses a trunk
I'd never worn
the apron they'd not believe
if I told them where
I buried the ring
they checked   the box
                     next to quiet

they named
my womb
Tender.

SOUTHWESTERN LUNATIC ASYLUM—VA

REPORT OF NEW PATIENT

Name, ... *Rachel Wells* ....

Received, ... *March 12* ...., 190...

Ward, No. ...... *6* ....; Room, No. .... *12* ....

Bath Given, ... ✓ ...; Enema Given, ...; Hair Cut, ... *shaved* ....

Body: Cleanly, ...; Filthy, ... ✓ ....; Vermin, ... ✓ ....

Wounds, Bruises, Sores, Swelling, Eruptions,&c., ...

...... *right jaw swollen* ....

....

Deformities, ... *No* ....

....

Weight, ... *143* .... pounds; Height, ... *5* .... feet...... *4* .... ins.

Ate the following, ... *refused tea and bread* ....

....

Mental Condition : Excited, ...; Talkative, ...

Quiet, ... ✓ ....; Obstinate, ...

Remarks: ... *asking for her baby* ....

....

....

I was present when the above patient was bathed and made in person the examination.

.... *M. A. Bolling* ....,

Matron.   Supervisor.

THEY CALL ME FILTHY, COVERED IN VERMIN

These bugs I carry
The ones I once fought
I shaved the boys' heads
But hers I could not
Day after day after day
I went through her hair
Pulled strand by strand
Through the split nail
Of my index finger
There was no such thing as time
Only the click   click   click
As I flicked the bugs out
Only my hand resting on her head.

MARRIAGE

I confess I felt trapped
From the first week
I fell into a malaise
Quite deep
They all talked about me
But I had no one
When the sickness came
It felt a relief.

TENDENCIES: KNIVES

Last night she yanked us from our slots
And stuffed us into a paper sack again
We don't know what she wants
To keep us from.

ANSWERED LETTERS

Dear Sir

She is right troublesome
and at times excited

We do not know whether or not she will ever improve

        Neither do we promise
        a cure

DEPOSITION

COUNTY OF TAZEWELL, TO-WIT:

Deposition of witnesses taken before us....*R. A. Williamson and Dr. J. J. Lowe* .... now sitting upon the examination of ......*Emma Darby*...... suspected of lunacy.

The deposition of ......*Daniel Darby*... being by us first duly sworn, in answer to the following interrogatories under oath, sayeth:

Name of patient? Answer, ...*Emma Darby*......................

Color? Answer, ...*White*..

Where born? Answer, ...*Raven, VA*..................................

Age? Answer, ...*55*..

Present Residence? Answer, ...*Raven, VA*.........................

Occupation? Answer, ...*widow*...

Education? Answer, ...*can read and write*............................

Civil Condition? Answer, ...*not neat in appearance*.................

Number of children had, if female? Answer, ...*3*...............

Name and address of guardian, nearest friend or relative?

Answer, ...*Daniel Darby, son*..

Is the patient addicted to the intemperate use of intoxicating liquors, tobacco, or drugs, or guilty of any injurious, improper, or immoral habit? State to what extent.

Answer, ... *chaws tobacco* ....

....

State fully and in detail any physical symptoms, injury, or disease from which the patient is at present suffering including, if any, female irregularities, and so forth, of menstruation?

Answer, ...*does nothing but sit with a looking glass in one hand & a brush in the other primping and powdering her face, has passed menopause*

SETTLING IN

Evenings they flock to my room
Broken toys
Doll heads dangling
They seek advice
They want me to fix it.

PLEASE

My things
Hoops
Frames
Floss
Before I took
To bed
Pins
Needles
Both
Tapestry and chenille
I made a living
Off my sewing
Please
Won't someone fetch
My things.

PATIENT RECORD

I. Mattie M. Roberts, age 19 years

Single, just from school
her father has considerable
property and his daughter here
as a pay patient
constantly moving
and throwing herself about
no restraint
has been imposed

II. Rachel Wells, age 32 years

Has had four children
her derangement
is chiefly hatred
of marriage
and religion
one of her children died
from drinking whiskey
and turpentine

III. Emma Darby, age 55 years

Widowed
has no property
asks frequently
for her sewing needles
and shears
difficult often
to be influenced
in any way
her disease appears
to increase

WHAT I LEFT BEHIND

1 scrubbing brush

1 kettle

3 dishcloths

1 bar carbolic soap

1 enamel bowl

2 packets ammonia

1 broom

1 husband

3 sons

~~1 daughter~~

PLEAS FOR RELEASE

My son, will you arrange for my release
　　I was widowed at 40 and lost everything
Oh father, will you arrange for my release
　　I was betrayed by one who ought to have protected me
Dear husband, will you arrange for my release
　　I was overcome with grief to think of our daughter's sufferings.

SLOW HEAT

High strung
They called her
Unsettled
We come home
She'd clawed her a notch
Jerked the planks right out
Said the witch needed her.

Ginseng they said
Ease the hippo
Help her sleep
Start slow
Build the dose
None of us knew
What it would take
To smother her.

Part Two: Treatment

I treasure more than ever a big darning needle I have—as nurses could at any moment remove any and all effects from my room, I keep this one possession by using it as a hairpin.

—Women of the Asylum

THE BEFORE TIME

Each time I came to
There were more people
In the room
They fell to their knees
Spoke in tongues
Lined out hymns
Granny brought 'sang
For my female weakness
She said but still I could not
Get out of bed

Used to be
I'd go with her
I had a quick eye
For all manner of roots
And kept my wits about me
In the woods
Now I ask for catmint
To calm my nerves
For cohosh to ease
The cramps
The nurses mumble
And bring more bromide
They curse and spit
The word Witch
Then leave the room
Before I can ask again.

NURSE VISITS

Shh

    I hissed   Shh
    Right in her face

Shh

    She would not Shh

Shh

    I could not   Shh

TENDING THE BABY

Makes me shake
And cry
I am well when away
And sick at home
I make a rag baby
Hang it from a doorknob
I crawl into closets
And under beds
There is no dementia
The doctor says
Only hysteria.

PATIENT INTERVIEW

My little girl is starving
Day and night
I plead
She needs food
Can't you hear her crying.

DOUBLE V

A bonnet   for my girl
The yarn   spun blue
At rest   she lies
Beyond   calm
Ribbons   woven
Choke   sky
I can't hold the scissors
Tight enough they slip
slice the seam unravels
Time pools in my hands

I MEASURE TIME

I measure time by the click
Of the speculum that shiny
Pretty thing (the click click)
I count the   click
As it opens me

DOCTOR VISITS

One of us fussed
Another complained
He shushed us with cotton
Tampons saturated in glycerin

One of us sang a right pretty tune
Another bickered with her tubes
One clamped down on his fingers
Another sputtered blood in his face
He swore he'd cure us all with a daily salt douche

One tilted, tried to hide
Another shed her skin each time he went in
Some had long been empty
Most were full   full of jewels
Full   of pins
One held the watch and chain
He lost back in 1910.

FEBRUARY

We wait for bedtime
Close the curtains
To make death come quicker.

THE INCIDENT: NOON

(The Record said)   I struggled
    And resisted
    And ran my stomach
        Into walls

(The Record said)   I screamed
    I'd kill the baby
    Or make myself go
        Into labor

The Record said

SOUTHWESTERN LUNATIC ASYLUM

Get me out
They cry day after day
Get me out
Of this place

They walk too heavy
Their voices swell my rooms
Disturbed
Leprous
Sick
They should know to tiptoe
They should know to speak in whispers

My walls throb
I absorb their wounds
Hold them until darkness descends.

SOON

Soon I'll hold
     Her
     Soon
Now it's only my knees
     I cradle
     And rock

BATH RULES

1)   Under

                      no circumstances
                      is a Patient to be bathed
    unless   two Attendants are
    present.

2)   In preparing a Bath the cold water is to be turned on first.

3)   Not more than one

                      Patient is to be bathed in the same
    water.

4)   No   brush of any kind
                      should be employed
                      in bathing a
    Patient.

5)   Under   no pretext
                      is the Patient's head
                      to be put under
    water.

ANSWERED LETTERS

Dear Sir
               Your daughter
                              Your wife
               Your mother

Has not improved any

PLEAS FOR RELEASE

My husband was murdered
     Will you arrange for my release
My baby died
     Will you arrange for my release
My father betrayed me
     Will you arrange for my release.

Part Three: Release

To escape, if possible, from the terrible shadowy something constantly haunting me, whose influence made itself felt in my happiest moments, giving character even to my dreams, and whose climax was insanity!

—From Under the Cloud

COVER THE MIRRORS,

I told them
On and on they hollered
In prayer
Their palms pressed
Oil to my forehead
     I'll fly away oh glory
     I'll fly away in the morning ...
They faked my healing
I cannot account for what evil
May enter.

RECREATION

Time was I knew
All the love ditties
And sang them too
Even though the church folk
Did not approve.

When the singers came
I was ready
>   *Got to go up*
>   *Time I was called up*
I flew, fell
Out the back door
Scrambled over the wall
My arms reached
For an endless horizon.

WHAT I BECAME

Quim-whiskers
Mossy treasure
Parsley bed
Plush
Love seat
Cock trap
Front parlour
That thing
Snapped shut

IN THE SEWING ROOM

Herringbone
Ripple
Lazy loth
French knot
By day I stitch
With the tapestry needle
I'm allowed.

At night the crewel
And chenille are mine
It's hard not to look at them
I rub them instead
Smooth   so smooth
I feel them shine.

PSYCHICAL EXAMINATION

FACIAL EXPRESSION __ *Blank* _____

MODE OF SPEECH—accelerated, ~~retarded~~, <u>incoherent</u>, &c.,

MANNER—excited, restless, active, ~~quiet~~ &c.,

CONDUCT—as to person and dress, ___ *Untidy* _____

GENERAL FEELING AND EMOTIONS—~~depressed~~, stuporous, <u>apathetic</u>, anxious, exalted, changeable, ~~irritable, &c.,~~

ATTENTION in conversation and to what is going on, ___ *Poor* _____

DELUSIONS (systemized or unsystemized), hallucinations or illusions—character, _____

MEMORY—as to recent or remote events, _____

ATTITUDE—towards self, others or environments, ___ *Suicidal* _____
Unconsciousness, _____ ; Sleep, _____

WILL, PLANS AND PURPOSES. Ideas accelerated, persistent, ~~retarded, rambling, &c.,~~

CAUSE OF DEATH, ___ *swallowing pins, needles, buttons, to which she was much addicted* _____

ANSWERED LETTERS

Dear Sir

She has much to try her temper

      In our opinion
                  She is yet

very insane

PATIENT INTERVIEW

Do you have visions
Hear voices
Did you drink in the darkness
See how bright it fills you?

ALL THE ONES I DO NOT SEE

I saw a mother open her mouth and eat
The doll whole
     That woman was not (me)
And I saw the man who was her father
He put the baby in her but he was not   (me)

          All the ones I do not see

I saw someone's daughter claw the leeches from her vagina
That girl was not   (me)
And I was not the doctor who opened her
Swam those fuckers in and then went
To supper

          All the ones I do not see

I saw the widow who sat before the mirror
But that woman was not   (me)
I saw the son who admitted her and heard him plea
She does nothing but primp and deplore her condition
But he was not me

          All the ones I do not see
          In the asylum
          They call to   me

PLEAS FOR RELEASE

We were
deranged on jealousy
We were
disposed to violence
We were
disinclined to do anything
We were
dissatisfied with everything.

RELEASE

The minister says I'm alive
Through grace says
They may never know
What rendered me silent
He tells them to pray
The spirit gives several messages
In other tongues
> *Praise the Lord*
> They shout
> *Praise the Lord*
The women place a Bible
Under my pillow I dream
My voice returns
I point to the minister
But no one listens.

E.H. ROBERTS

October 3, 19_____

Richlands, VA

My dear Sir:

Have a Commission of Lunacy summoned at once and have Mattie examined and send in depositions, and we will re-admit her soon as possible. There is room. We are surprised as she had no marked incidents of insanity for over 12 months.

Yours truly,
Robert J. Preston, Supt.

By Z.V.S. Asst. Phyn.

THE INCIDENT: MORNING

I found the stockings you gave her
And that dress so frilly
Did you tell her to keep them
     Nice and pressed
Did you tell her to keep them
     For her burial.

HAIR

Once sun touched
From the tops of trees
Now it comes out
By handfuls
I crochet into baby blankets
At night I gather strands
In the corner
See I am here
Please tell them
I was here.

ARRIVAL

God save me. God could not. Safe here away from him, or nearer. A door. Another (door after door) and I open. I open my bags. They've emptied (me). They've taken her. God (be with me) let me keep the baby. I've not had time to finish her blanket. The final door. Open(s).

NOTES

These poems are inspired by research into the 1887–1948 patient records of Southwestern State Hospital (formerly Southwestern Lunatic Asylum and currently operating as Southwestern Virginia Mental Health Institute) housed at the Library of Virginia. In particular,

1. Series IV, Letter Books and Correspondence Records, Superintendent's Letter Book, 1901.

2. Series VI, Patient Records, 1887–1918.

    a. Case Book, Female (Number 1), 1887–1890
    b. Clinical Record, Female (Number 8), 1907–1915
    c. Record of Clothing and Valuables Received from Patients, 1903–1917

And by reading secondary sources:

Agnew, Agnes. *From Under the Cloud*. Robert Clark & Co, 1886.

Black, Edwin. *War Against the Weak: Eugenics and America's Campaign to Create a Master Race*. Dialog Press, 2003.

Ehrenreich, Barbara & Deirdre English. *For Her Own Good: Two Centuries of the Experts' Advice to Women*. Second Anchor Books Edition, 2005.

Geller, Jeffrey L. and Maxine Harris. *Women of the Asylum: Voices from Behind the Walls, 1840–1945*. Anchor Books, 1994.

Johnson, Carla. "The Perception and Treatment of Insanity in Southern Appalachia" (2012). Electronic Theses and Dissertations.

Light, Phyllis D. *Southern Folk Medicine*. North Atlantic Books, 2018.

McCauley, Deborah Vansau. *Appalachian Mountain Religion: A History*. U of Illinois, 1995.

Out of Her Mind: Women Writing on Madness, Ed. Rebecca Shannonhouse. Modern Library Edition, 2003.

Payne, Christopher. *Asylum: Inside the Closed World of State Mental Hospitals*. MIT Press, 2009.

Penney, Darby & Peter Stastny. *The Lives They Left Behind: Suitcases from a State Hospital Attic*. Bellevue Literary Press, 2008.

Washburn, Benjamin Earle. *A Country Doctor in the Southern Mountains.* Spindale Press, 1955.

In the end, these poems are imaginary works. The characters in this book are fictitious. Any similarity to real persons, living or dead, is coincidental and not intended by the author.

ACKNOWLEDGMENTS

The author gratefully acknowledges the publications in which versions of the following poems first appeared.

Still: The Journal: "Double V"; "They call me filthy, covered in vermin"; "Hair"

Pen+Brush: "Tendencies: Knives"; "Arrival"; "What I Became"; "Answered Letters"; "Bath Rules"; "There is Room"

South Florida Poetry Journal: "Answered Letters"

SWWIM Every Day: "All the Ones I Do Not See"

The Disappointed Housewife: "Arrival"; "What I Became"; "What I Left Behind"; "There Is Room"; "Bath Rules"

Hellscape Press: "The Incident: Noon"; "The Incident: Morning"; "Tendencies: Knives"

Workhorse Gauntlet & Women Speak: "Doctor Visits" (as "On Women, Their Bodies")

Literary Accents: "Marriage"; "The day they came for me"; "Patient Interview"

Appalachian Review: "Testimony;" "Slow Heat"; "Release" (as "Redemption"); "Cover the mirrors"

Mom Egg Review: "Tending the baby"

★★

Thank you to the Kentucky Foundation for Women for funding the research that gave voice to these poems.

Thank you to Christopher McCurry and the Workhorse Poetry Gauntlet for the community that nurtured this project.

Thank you to Katerina Stoykova and Accents Publishing for bringing this book to the world.

Thank you to Shari Weschler for the conversations about art and the generous gift of her painting for the cover.

Thank you to Rachael White for her close attention to editing this book.

Thank you to my family for being by my side.

ABOUT THE AUTHOR

Tina Parker is the author of two previous poetry collections, *Mother May I* and *Another Offering*. Her current work springs from historical research into the lives of women labeled as "other"—whether that be witch, insane, or hysterical. The poems in *Lock Her Up* stem from 19th and 20th century patient records of Southwestern Lunatic Asylum in Marion, Virginia. Tina grew up in nearby Bristol, Virginia, and now lives in Berea, Kentucky. To learn more about her work, visit *www.tina-parker.org*, or follow her on Instagram *@tetched_poet*.

CPSIA information can be obtained
at www.ICGtesting.com
Printed in the USA
JSHW021909120921
18655JS00002B/99